A Collection
for Healing and Self-Empowerment

A Warriors Reminder

Ash Alves

A Warriors Reminder- A Collection of Reminders for Healing and Self-Empowerment. All rights reserved. Copyright © 2021 "Ashanty Alves" Ash Alves. No part of this publication may be reproduced, photocopied, or shared in any form without the prior written consent of the publisher except for the use of quotations in a book review.

ISBN 9781086198157

Imprint: Independently published

Website: www.ashalvesblog.com
Instagram: ashalves_
Pinterest: ashalves_

Organisation: Warrior Reminder

Editor: Tols Abeni
Designer: Ash Alves
Photographer: Thato Matsose

'When I dare to be powerful, to use my strength in the service of my vision, then it becomes less and less important whether I'm afraid.' - Audre Lorde

Contents

Introduction	7
Warrior.	11
Patience.	13
Presence.	15
Feel the fear.	17
Give yourself permission.	19
Surrender.	21
Wounds into wisdom.	23
Lovable.	25
Celebrate your wins.	27
Transition is a part of life.	29
Change.	31
The best time is now.	33
You can't change people.	35
Trust your inner wisdom.	37
New beginnings.	39
You deserve to shine.	41
Creativity and Social Media.	43
Forgive yourself.	45
Self-care.	47

Uniqueness.	49
Obstacles.	51
Power of the tongue.	53
Material possessions.	55
Feel your feelings.	57
Validation.	59
Highly sensitive.	61
Values.	63
Narratives.	65
Gratitude.	67
Coping mechanisms.	69
The art of saying no.	71
Self-awareness.	73
Expand your horizon.	75
Evolving.	77
Differences.	79
Endings.	81
Oppression.	83
Solitude.	85
Failure.	87
Healing.	89
Unconditional.	91
Enjoy the ride.	93

Unexpected changes.	95
Driver's seat.	97
Unapologetic.	99
Expectations.	101
Progress not perfection.	103
Authenticity.	105
Learning.	107
Faith.	109
Codependent.	111
Intergenerational trauma.	113
Overthinking.	115
Acknowledgments	116

Introduction

When your back is against the wall, there are only two options available- you either give up or fight. In 2017, I chose to fight. I decided that I was going to do everything in my power to feel better about myself. At rock bottom, I found the courage to face myself and take action on the chaos that surrounded me.

My first introduction to healing began through writing. Journaling was the first time I dared to examine myself. As I began to uncover the layers of trauma and negative thinking, I realised how much pain I had carried for many years. Unearthing and exposing my pain allowed for transformation and healing to emerge. I discovered my true self, the one that existed beyond the pain. I rediscovered my voice. By giving myself permission to explore, feel, and release, I started to like myself again. I realised that I had the power to effect change in my life. I realised that I don't have to do it alone as I am always and protected by the divine. I realised that no matter how difficult life gets, there's always an opportunity to rise and start again. Journaling drew my attention to a fundamental thing that was in my control and that is my perspective. I realised that perspective is the gateway towards self-actualisation.

I began to see life's tragedies and so-called coincidences that I had experienced as lessons I had to go through to help me become the highest version of self. I used my pain as an opportunity for self-examination and healing. I was no longer merely a victim to life but a victor- standing tall in the face of adversity and becoming a better person because of it.

I began sharing my writings online because I wanted to open up about the struggles I had experienced and no longer wanted to live in shame. I met a community of people who were embarking on a healing journey. I also encountered people who had lost their way and desperately wanted guidance on how to get back to feeling better about life again. It was through my encounters that I realised that so many people suffer in silence, yet many have similar experiences. I decided to start recording the lessons I was learning on my journey, hoping that it may help someone else in need of extra guidance.

This book is an opportunity to share pieces of the lessons I have learned so far on my journey. My goal is to help inspire you to experience life differently. I am also here to remind you that you were put on this earth to thrive, not suffer. I want you to realise that change is readily available to you and that you are not bound to a life of misery. How you think about yourself and the world can change if you dare to look within yourself. I am here to guide you towards your inner healer and support you in becoming the best version of you.

A Warriors Reminder should be used as a tool for self-examination and exploration. It is an opportunity to examine life's issues and to heal the landscape of your inner thoughts and feelings. The messages within this book can be used as inspiration to support you in dismantling old thought patterns and replacing them with new, life-affirming ones. Seeing universal life issues from a fresh perspective allows you to create a deeper awareness of yourself and the process of life.

I invite you to give yourself permission to want something new and ask that you open yourself up to seeing things from a new perspective. When we become devoted to healing our inner world, loving and honouring ourselves, and using that love as a standard by which we interact with others, we gain greater self-love and gratitude for life.

How to use this book?

This book is created for everyday use and made for you to revisit. I would suggest using it practically by engaging with the reminders in this book through journaling. You can choose a topic that resonates with you and use the journal prompts as a reflective practice.

Here are some ways you can use this book:

- Choose a topic and use the journal prompt. Reflect on your experiences in this area.
- Go into a quiet room and ask your intuition for guidance on the positive shifts you want to make in your life and then choose a random page in the book.
- Discuss the book with your peer group or a friend.

Ultimately, I urge you to use this book in a way that resonates with you. Test out the words of encouragement offered and explore the new understandings you have developed. I wish you a safe journey back to yourself.

Love Ash,

Ash Alves

I am a warrior. I have the courage, strength and power to overcome any adversity that comes my way.

Warrior.

Remind yourself of what you've been able to overcome. All the times you felt like you weren't going to make it through, you proved yourself wrong. You're more powerful than you think.

Journal Prompt: What's one obstacle that you've overcome recently?

Doors are getting ready to open for me.

Patience.

We live in a microwave generation where we expect instant gratification. However, some things take time to build. If you are currently not where you want to be, trust that it will work out. It might take you longer than others to achieve your goals, but if you continue to do the work towards your goals and stay consistent, you will inevitably get to where you want to be. Just like a flower, the seeds don't blossom overnight, but require nurturing and patience to see their beautiful potential. Have more faith in your journey and remember that what is to come will be amazing.

Journal Prompt: What area of your life requires more patience?

Being present allows me to become an
active co-creator of my reality.

Presence.

Being present reassures that your actions and intentions are aligned with your highest and greater good. We navigate life running on autopilot, letting our conscious and unconscious thought patterns control our actions. We react to what is going on around us instead of operating from a place of mindfulness. Being present allows you to take your power back. Awareness of the present allows you to take control over your actions and live more intentionally. Tap into the now and be present as you navigate through life.

Journal Prompt: What is your intention for today?

Make your vision more powerful than your fears.

Feel the fear.

Try a 'feel the fear and do it anyway' approach. Accept that the fear exists and don't try to resist it. Fear is a natural emotion that even the most successful people experience. It's when we allow fear to stop us from achieving our goals that it begins to hinder us. Use fear as fuel to pursue your goals, even if you're scared, because you might end up blocking a blessing from entering your life. It's better to move with fear, than to stop and always wonder what your life would have looked like if you made the move.

Journal Prompt: What will your life look like if decide to go after your dreams?

I give myself permission to show up in the world as my authentic self. I don't need a co-sign to be the person the divine intends me to be in this life.

Give yourself permission.

If you always wait for others to give you permission to do something that you've been wanting to do, then you might be waiting for a long time. You must encourage yourself to do things in the same way that you would encourage a friend. You are wise enough, talented enough, and smart enough to be great at what you want to achieve. Society and people may tell you different, but there's always room for you. Live your life as a demonstration to others that with belief in self, all things are possible.

Journal Prompt: What do you need to give yourself permission to want in life?

Sometimes you've got to surrender
so you can be open to receive.

Surrender.

Be willing to accept that things were supposed to happen the way they did whether or not you can understand why. You may be aching over the intricate details, fighting against the pain and devastation it has caused you. If you keep battling with reality, you will always end up losing. Let go of your attachment to what you think should have happened and surrender to what is right now. You may not know where you're heading but trust that you're being guided towards a place that serves you well.

Journal Prompt: What does your soul want to surrender?

My wounds are markers of how much I've overcome and my ability to turn a negative situation into a valuable life lesson.

Wounds into wisdom.

No matter the depth of your pain, there's something you can pull from your experience- whether that's grief connecting you to the preciousness of life or heartbreak reminding you of the importance of self-love. You can draw your own meaning from pain to encourage you to keep going. Your wounds are not a hindrance but are markers of what you've been through and how much you've overcome. Affirm today that your pain will not define you but will make you a better, wiser, stronger, and more compassionate person.

Journal Prompt: What lessons have you learned from your pain?

You are worthy of love. You deserve everything that has been nurtured by love. Forgive yourself for the times you allowed yourself to believe otherwise.

Lovable.

You may have encountered experiences that made you feel like you're not worthy of love. Perhaps you may feel like you have to change who you are or lower your standards to be loved. Disempower that voice inside that tells you that you're not worthy of love. Instead of pouring so much energy into feeling disappointed by how they treated you, give yourself the love you expect from others.

Journal Prompt: How can you show yourself love?

Celebrate yourself every time you
achieve a milestone, large or small.

Celebrate your wins.

Celebrate your successes no matter how large or small. When you become your own cheerleader, you motivate yourself to continue taking progressive steps forward. Celebrating yourself is a way you honour who you are and what you've worked hard to achieve. Pat yourself on the back more often because you deserve praise. All your successes are showing you what you're capable of when you put your mind to it.

Journal Prompt: What's one of your greatest achievements?

I will take on any transitional phase with ease. Even if I can't make sense of it all right now, I trust that everything will align for my highest and greater good.

Transition is a part of life.

You may not understand the chain of events or the transitional phase that you're currently going through right now. You may be unsure whether things will work out in your best interest. Note to self: not understanding your current circumstances is completely normal. Sometimes life requires you to ride the wave and take it one day at a time. Although things might not be clear to you now, they will be eventually. Transition creates space for something greater and more profound to take place. Uncomfortable change makes room transformation to occur. Personal growth arrives when you embrace change and allow it to transform you.

Journal Prompt: What words of reassurance can you offer yourself right now?

Don't be afraid to reintroduce yourself to people.

Change.

You are not the person you used to be. Don't be afraid to tell people that you've changed. Your boundaries look different. Your outlook looks different. You are not tolerating what you used to. You are walking on a path of purpose and conviction. Reintroduce yourself so they get to know the new you.

Journal Prompt: How have you changed over the last five years?

I can begin building the life of my dreams right now using the resources that are currently available to me.

The best time is now.

A lot of us tend to stall ourselves under the guise of waiting for the right time. Having a set strategy behind your ultimate goal is paramount. However, sometimes we get stuck in the planning phase, convincing ourselves that we aren't ready when we already have all of the tools available for us to start. If you keep waiting for the right time to pursue your dreams, you might be waiting forever. The best time is now. Don't underestimate your ability to go after what you want, using the tools that are currently available to you.

Journal Prompt: What action steps can you take towards achieving your goals this week?

I make a commitment to stop trying to change those who are unwilling to change themselves. I accept them for who they are and choose to pour my energy into people who respect, love and appreciate me.

You can't change people.

You can't force someone to change unless they're willing to help themselves. Trying to change people who have shown you their unwillingness to do so is a waste of energy. As much as it may hurt, you must free them from your own expectations. Their inability to change is a reflection of them not you. You break your own heart when you continue waiting and wishfully hoping that people will make the necessary changes for you. Learn to accept what you cannot control and protect your energy if needed.

Journal Prompt: What do you need to accept about someone that you've been resisting?

You don't need to seek advice for everything. The answers often lay within you. Trust your inner wisdom.

Trust your inner wisdom.

The answers that we often seek outside of ourselves exists within us. Taking on too many opinions can affect how you see yourself and lead you towards following a path in life that is not your own. With the wrong advice, we can become disheartened and doubt that we've got what it takes to make the right decisions. Your intuition is guiding you. When you ignore your inner wisdom, you're sending a message that you don't trust yourself. Put more faith in yourself and trust that your inner wisdom will guide you to places that serve you well.

Journal Prompts: What is your intuition telling you that you've been ignoring?

The sun rises and sets to remind us that
everyday we have an opportunity to start again.

New beginnings.

Every day is an opportunity to transform our lives and learn from our past mistakes. Take a moment when you first wake up to remind yourself that you are in control of how you choose to live your life. Make a commitment to handling challenges head on and to change the things you can control.

Journal Prompt: What are you going to do differently today?

I possess the skills, passion and drive to thrive in my chosen career path. I deserve to occupy space.

You deserve to shine.

There are probably millions of people passionate about similar things as you. This can feel intimidating and make us question whether we've got what it takes to thrive in our pursuits. However, you have something special to offer simply by being you. Your uniqueness is what sets you apart from others. You possess the skills and passion that can make you a valuable asset to your field. Remember that you're worthy of taking up space.

Journal Prompt: What impact do you want to make in the world?

I am a creative being and what I choose to create is good enough.

Creativity and Social Media.

Creativity is how you draw meaning from life. It connects you to your inner child. It's a way you practice joy and experience the pleasures of being alive. We live in an age where social media provides us with a platform for us to showcase our creativity. Yet our creative work gets valued based on likes, popularity, and co-signs by blue tick pages. We often feel that we must cater our creativity to what is expected, what is considered the norm and therefore manufacture something that doesn't align with our inner joy. Creativity becomes a chore rather than a way to connect with being alive. Don't let these human-made algorithms control you. Your creativity is worthy and it's yours to define. Create because it feeds your soul. Create for the love of creating. Stay grounded and remind yourself of your intentions so that you don't get swept away by what everyone else is doing.

Journal Prompt: What do you get lost doing that brings you joy?

I forgive myself for believing that my past mistakes define who I am and all that I will become.

Forgive yourself.

When you keep score of all the mistakes you made in the past, you will only end up feeling crap about yourself. If you can forgive others for their shortcomings then why can't you forgive yourself? It's time to forgive yourself for the decisions you made that don't align with your higher self. The past version of you does not know the lessons you know now. Not even our greats are immune from making mistakes. Remember this- your life will ultimately be determined by how you used your shortcomings to become a better person.

Journal Prompt: What do you need to forgive yourself for?

Self-care is productive.

Self-care.

Self-care is a radical act in a world that applauds overworking and demands your servitude to a market-based economy. Looking after your mental, physical, spiritual, and emotional wellbeing is an act of self-preservation. Self-care looks like saying no, setting boundaries, surrounding yourself with good company, connecting with your joy or resting. When you are feeling your best, it benefits how you show up for others.

Journal Prompt: What can you do to look after yourself better?

I embrace my uniqueness and choose not to conceal it for the comfortability of others.

Uniqueness.

Never compromise who you are to fit in. It is precisely your uniqueness that makes you awesome. Imagine how boring the world would be if everyone succumbed to the pressures of society's expectations. The world needs more people who are daring enough to be themselves. You may encounter people who aren't going to embrace you, but you'll also meet many who find value in who you are. Life is too short to mould yourself into something that you're not.

Journal Prompt: What's your favourite thing about your personality?

This too shall pass.

Obstacles.

Progress is not a linear process. It can be frustrating when we feel like we are making progress but then something happens that takes us off track. First and foremost, you're not alone in feeling like this. We all have these moments when life's struggles get the best of us. Life comes with bumps in the road and sometimes you're going to experience unexpected obstacles along the way. Be persistent in your efforts and remind yourself that this obstacle won't last forever.

Journal Prompt: What obstacles have you overcome recently?

I choose words that honour my existence. I speak life into myself daily.

Power of the tongue.

Be mindful of how you talk about yourself in front of others. If you are putting yourself down more than you are affirming yourself, you may be sending a message of how you treat yourself. Say good things about yourself. Give yourself credit where it's due. If you're telling yourself and others that you're 'stupid' and 'silly', people are unconsciously picking up on how you treat yourself which may, in turn, affect how they treat you. Your words have power. Use them wisely.

Journal Prompt: What unkind words are you using towards yourself that you want to let go of?

My worth is not determined by material possessions. I was born worthy.

Material possessions.

Your worth is not determined by material possessions. In the age of social media and celeb culture, it's easy to fall into the trap of constantly wanting new possessions to make you feel satisfied. However, material possessions can't fill the void that's within you. No amount of material items will be enough until you fundamentally believe that you are enough. You are inherently worthy, and you don't need to have more of anything to begin loving who you are.

Journal Prompt: What unhealthy attachments do you need to let go of?

I am courageous enough to
hold space to feel my pain.

Feel your feelings.

When you are feeling negative emotions, don't resist them. Allow yourself the space to feel a range of emotions no matter how uncomfortable they may feel. Suppressing your feelings only creates unresolved pain. Your heart may ache for many days, even years. The pain can feel so excruciating and feel like there's no end in sight. It's not easy to sit with ourselves during moments of discomfort but by surrendering, we allow our emotions to pass through us. Having an open and honest conversation with yourself is the first step towards healing. Once you feel your feelings, healing can take place. Feel it, acknowledge it, and address it. The only way is through.

Journal Prompt: What feelings are you avoiding and why are you afraid to feel it?

No amount of validation will be enough
until I decide to validate myself.

Validation.

No one can fill the void that's within you but you. You can have people around you who admire and love you, but until you accept yourself, no amount of praise from others will be enough. Anyone else's positive opinion of you should simply add to your pre-existing belief system. When you rely on others to see your worth, you give them the power to remove it. Your worth is not contingent upon people's ability to see it.

Journal Prompt: How can you validate yourself more often?

My sensitivity is a superpower.

Highly sensitive.

Being highly sensitive is a superpower. The ability to be considerate, compassionate, and aware truly makes you a blessing to humanity. Don't let people gaslight you and make you feel bad for being who you are. You don't need to change. In fact, the world needs to adjust to your kind nature.

Journal Prompt: What are the positives of being highly sensitive?

A Warriors Reminder

My values are non-negoitable.

Values.

Never compromise your values. A person who stands for nothing stands for anything. When you send a clear message about what you want and are willing to accept, opportunities meet you where you are at. If respect matters, don't settle for anyone who treats you less than you deserve. Values ensure that your daily actions are in alignment with your highest and greater good. It allows you to attract what you truly want in life.

Journal Prompt: What are your values?

I let go of any narratives that no longer
serve the person I am becoming.

Narratives.

The narratives you tell yourself have power. If you tell yourself that you can't do something, then you most likely won't. If you can't take responsibility for yourself and your life, you will find yourself in situations that disrupt your peace. When you begin to let go of the narratives you hold onto, you'll begin to see the trajectory of your life start to change. You will begin to go from powerless to powerful. You may have been a victim in the past but the choice to stay in victimhood is yours. Choose to take ownership over your life.

Journal Prompt: What narratives are you holding onto that disempower you?

I express gratitude daily and give
thanks for all the blessings in my life.

Gratitude.

Make it a daily practice to reflect on what you are grateful for in life. Showing gratitude makes us realise that there is so much to be thankful for beyond our current circumstances. When you shift your focus on appreciating the things that you have rather than what you lack, you invite more abundance into your life.

Journal Prompt: What are you grateful for today?

I forgive myself for the unhealthy
ways I dealt with my pain when I
didn't know any other way.

Coping mechanisms.

Sometimes the pain feels so difficult to hold that a person may turn towards unhealthy coping mechanisms to run away from it. You may feel guilty for how you've hurt yourself or others. It's important to offer yourself self-compassion by recognising that your actions came from a hurt place. Acknowledge that if you had the resources that are available to you now, you would have done better back then. Despite your shortcomings, know that you're not judged and are unconditionally loved by God.

Journal Prompt: What coping mechanisms have you been using to mask your pain?

'No' is a complete sentence.

The art of saying no.

You don't have to compromise your needs and desires to please others. The beauty of saying 'no' is that it allows you to filter out all the things that aren't in alignment with the type of life you want to live. It also helps you to avoid putting yourself in uncomfortable situations. Although saying no can make us feel uneasy and worried about upsetting others, it is necessary to preserve our integrity and personal interests. Make decisions that are in alignment with your inner needs and desires.

Journal Prompt: What do you need to say no to in your life?

Self-awareness is how I take my power back.

Self-awareness.

Painful past experiences, if not healed from, get stored in the body and end up becoming negative core beliefs. You may find yourself unconsciously attracting unhealthy relationships or perhaps sabotaging good opportunities because you believe you're not good enough. You are not a bad person for falling into negative patterns and doing things that don't support your growth. However, once you've acknowledged your patterns, you must unlearn them. It will be difficult and may take plenty of time, but you're more than capable of breaking the cycle. Ask for the help you need if you are struggling. You don't have to do it alone.

Journal Prompt: What are your unhealthy patterns?

My abundant life is outside
of my comfort zone.

Expand your horizon.

Take small steps to expand your horizon. If you don't push yourself beyond what you know, how will you ever find out what you can achieve? Allowing fear to stop you from taking risks only blocks potential blessings from entering your life. When we do the thing we are afraid of doing, we get used to a life of growth and expansion. You will find yourself in unimaginable places.

Journal Prompts: What's one thing you can do out of your comfort zone this week?

Honour your growth and never dim your light
for the comfortability of others. It is your
divine right to shine your light in the world.

Evolving.

Sometimes we feel guilty because the person we once were isn't who we are now. When we evolve, we move out of alignment with certain people around us. Stand proud in who you are. Honour your growth and never dim your light to make others comfortable. The people who are meant to be in your life will support you.

Journal Prompt: How have you changed in the last few years?

A Warriors Reminder

I accept others for who they are. I can guide and assist people but I can't change them. Everyone is an authority over themselves.

Differences.

Before we decide to judge others for their actions, we must first try to understand them. Not everyone is going to make choices you'll agree with or that align with your values. Remember that we are all navigating the world on different levels of consciousness. Let go of expecting that other people will act according to your perceptions of the world. If the differences impact your ability to show up as your true self and threaten your humanity, then you can decide to distance yourself, remove them or set boundaries.

Journal Prompt: What do you need to accept about someone in your life that you've been resisting?

A Warriors Reminder

I am deserving of reciprocal relationships
and connections with people who have
my best interest at heart.

Endings.

It's painful when you experience a relationship breakdown. If a relationship brings you more pain than joy, you must seriously consider whether it's worth maintaining. No matter what their relationship is with you, you do not deserve to be treated badly or feel like you must compromise your integrity to be around them. Ask yourself what you expect from the relationship and decide to put your needs and desires first. You can love people from a distance.

Journal Prompt: What does a healthy relationship, (platonic and/ or romantic) look like to you?

I have the power to create change
in my life and community.

Oppression.

It's important not to undermine the impacts that white supremacist, capitalist, imperialist patriarchy have on one's ability to self-actualise. Structural oppression can crush one's sense of hope and optimism. Despite the realities of oppression, hope and resilience can be found. We may have many obstacles to overcome but we can still choose to reclaim authority over lives. Whilst we work on unlearning and breaking the shackles in our minds and dismantling systems of oppression, we must pour our energy into what we can change.

Journal Prompt: What changes can you make that will benefit your wider community?

Quiet moments allow me to reach deep down
inside and listen to my heart's desires.

Solitude.

Cherish the moments that you get to spend alone. Being alone gives us space to tune into our needs and desires. When we are constantly stimulated in the presence of others, we can easily become disconnected internally. Being content with your silence allows you to develop greater self-love and awareness which will positively impact how you show up in the world and your relationships with others.

Journal Prompt: What are your quiet moments teaching you about yourself?

Failures are lessons and blessings in disguise. Failure prepares me to receive something more profound.

Failure.

You can't experience the fullness of what life has to offer you without failure. You have to be willing to fall flat on your face to create the life you want to live. Failure gives us a unique opportunity to learn from our mistakes and make better decisions. The difference between winners and losers is that a winner never gives up in the face of adversity. Every time you fall flat on your face, get back up. Treat those wounds as learning opportunities.

Journal Prompt: What lessons have come out of your failures?

I am kind and patient with
myself on this journey called life.

Healing.

Healing is not a linear process. Some days you are going to feel like giving up. Learn to hold yourself during those moments and give yourself permission to feel. Healing has its highs and lows. Your lows are part of the process towards greater transformation.

Journal Prompt: What are you currently healing from?

I am deserving of love even on the
days I don't quite love myself.

Unconditional.

Even on your worst days, you are loved. Even on the days when you find yourself reverting to old ways of being, you are loved. On the days where you want to give up, you are loved. On the days where you betray yourself, you are loved. Flaws and all, you are still loved. The divine creator doesn't require you to be perfect to be deemed lovable.

Journal prompt: What's one thing you love about yourself?

The journey is just as important
as achieving the goal itself.

Enjoy the ride.

The journey it takes us to reach our goals is just as important as the goal itself. It's through those steps that we learn about ourselves. All the bumps in the road will make for an awesome story to tell one day. So whilst you're embarking on your journey towards achieving your goals, don't forget to enjoy the ride.

Journal Prompt: What brings you joy?

It may not happen the way I want it to but it will happen the way it's supposed to. I remain open to adjustments and trust that I will be guided towards places that serve me well.

Unexpected changes.

You can do as much planning as you want, but nothing can prepare you for certain life experiences. Sometimes life hits us with surprises that we were not prepared for. Whilst planning, be flexible and be kind to yourself when things don't go according to plan.

Journal Prompt: What thoughts can bring you peace in moments of uncertainty?

I am in the driver's seat of my life.

Driver's seat.

It is easy to get so caught up in responding to our daily obligations that we begin to feel powerless in creating change within our lives. Your life to some degree is a physical manifestation of the choices you've made up to this date. We may not have control over everything that happens to us, but we get to decide how we allow those things to shape us. You are in the driver's seat of your life. Do not give anyone else the power to control the direction you take.

Journal Prompt: How can you take more control over your life?

A Warriors Reminder

I am the author of my life and I get to decide how I show up in the world.

Unapologetic.

Other people's perception of you is none of your business. You can't live your life trying to please everyone. No matter what you do, someone will find an excuse not like you. It's better to be yourself knowing you will attract authentic connections with people who respect and admire you. Your duty on this earth is to be your authentic self. Don't allow others to deter you from honouring what's true to you.

Journal Prompt: What opinions from others and society have you taken on that you want to let go of?

I am creating a beautiful life for myself and letting go of any expectations that no longer serve me.

Expectations.

You get to decide what success looks like to you. Be brave enough to live according to your rules and what resonates with you. If society's expectations don't reflect the type of life you want to live, then give yourself permission to let go. People are not living your life and won't have to bear the burden of living an unfulfilling existence. Live a life that you are proud of living.

Journal Prompt: What does success look like to you?

I choose progress over perfection.

Progress not perfection.

Healing is not about achieving perfection- it's about making progress. An obsession with personal development can have you thinking of yourself as a project that needs to be fixed. You're already whole. Healing is about becoming more of yourself. When you focus on perfection, you place unrealistic expectations on yourself. Progress is loving and kind, whilst trying to attain perfection means being harsh on yourself. Be kinder to yourself on your journey.

Journal Prompt: What area of your life are you making progress?

Being yourself is the greatest
gift you can offer the world.

Authenticity.

It takes courage to be yourself in a world where you are constantly told that who you are isn't enough. Being yourself is the greatest gift you can offer yourself and others. When you show up as your authentic self, you begin to attract people who value and appreciate who you are. You will start attracting what you want and start living a life that's in alignment with your highest good. Be brave enough to show the world who you are without an apology.

Journal Prompt: What does living authentically look like to you?

I am both a teacher and student of life.

Learning.

Don't be afraid to reach out for help if you are stuck on something and not sure what direction to take. Life is about learning. We are not going to know the answers to everything and that's okay. Become a student of life and utilise the resources around you to help guide you. Asking for help does not make you weak nor incapable. In fact, acknowledging that being a better version of yourself requires you to learn from others is a sign of your maturity. The person who thinks they know it all becomes stagnant because they are unable to see their limitations. Take all the resources you can and apply it to your own life.

Journal Prompt: What would you like to learn this year?

I have faith that all will be well, even if I can't see how it's going to come together yet.

Faith.

Having unwavering faith is the light at the end of the tunnel. With faith, we can make it through our hardest times. Faith is a knowing that things will eventually be okay even if we can't see nor understand how things are going to work out. Faith reminds us that we are unconditionally loved and protected by a source beyond ourselves.

Journal Prompt: How can having faith improve your life?

I break free from being emotionally enmeshed with others and choose to create healthy relationships.

Codependent.

Pay attention to what your unhealthy relationship dynamics are teaching you about yourself. You should know your value independent of others. You should be free to be your authentic self. You should be free to express your needs and desires without fearing that you won't be accepted. If you find yourself hiding who you are and absorbing other people's feelings, dig deeper and discover why you've become so emotionally enmeshed with others. You can unlearn these unhealthy patterns by getting clear about who you are, what you want, and giving yourself what you desperately seek in others.

Journal Prompt: What codependent relationships do you have in your life?

I am breaking the cycle of dysfunction for myself, community and future generations.

Intergenerational trauma.

You are breaking the cycle of intergenerational trauma. Each time you decide to heal yourself and do better, you're unlearning unhealthy patterns passed down through generations. You may fall short sometimes but you are still doing your best despite the pain that has been passed down to you. Never underestimate the impact that you are making.

Journal Prompt: What intergenerational traumas are you healing from?

I choose thoughts that serve me and let go of the rest.

Overthinking.

Overthinking steals you away from the present moment. Not everything requires a deep analysis. Some things will never be fully understood no matter how much we try to find the answers. Allow there to be holes in your knowledge. Life carries a certain mystery which we all must embrace and accept. Give yourself permission to live without overanalysing your behaviour and the environment around you. Release yourself from the shackles of your mind that keep you trapped in a cycle of self-doubt and worry.

Journal Prompt: What can you do to quieten your mind today?

Acknowledgments

Without the divine creator, this book would not have been possible. I give thanks to my ancestors and chosen guides for protecting me and showing me unconditional love.

My heartfelt gratitude to my younger sister Erykah Alves and soul friend, Chanel James for their support, wisdom, and guidance and for making it easier to be at home with myself.

To all my amazing friends, I thank you for your support and for inspiring me by shining your light. To the countless people who have supported me along the way, thank you for all your encouragement.

About the author

Ash Alves the founder of Warrior Reminder, a platform she created to empower and support people to heal and self-actualise. Besides running Warrior Reminder, she is also a writer, workshop facilitator and advocate. She graduated with a degree in International Politics from City University London. She lives in the West Midlands.

Made in the USA
Middletown, DE
26 November 2023

43513469R00073